Blue
Hour

ALSO BY CAROLYN FORCHÉ

Gathering the Tribes

The Country Between Us

The Angel of History

Against Forgetting: Twentieth-Century Poetry of Witness (Editor)

Blue
Hour

Carolyn Forché

HarperCollins*Publishers*

HarperCollins books may be purchased for educational, business, or sales promotional use. For information, please write: Special Markets Department, HarperCollins Publishers Inc., 10 East 53rd Street, New York, NY 10022.

FIRST EDITION

Designed by Nicola Ferguson

Printed on acid-free paper

Library of Congress Cataloging-in-Publication Data
Forché, Carolyn.
Blue Hour / by Carolyn Forché.—1st ed.
p. cm.
ISBN 0-06-009912-7
I. Title
PS3556.O68 B58 2003
811'.54—dc21   2002027270

03 04 05 06 07 ❖/PC 10 9 8 7 6 5 4 3 2 1

for Harry and Sean Christophe

I am deeply grateful to J. Patrick Lannan and Lannan Foundation for the support that made this book possible, and also to Robert and Peggy Boyers, editors of *Salmagundi*, where "Blue Hour" and "Nocturne" were originally published, and Michael Ondaatje and Linda Spalding, publishers of *Brick*, where "Afterdeath" and "Refuge" first appeared.

Contents

These moments are immortal, and most transitory of all; no content may be secured from them. . . . Beams of their power stream into the ordered world and dissolve it again and again.

—*Martin Buber*

Blue
Hour

Sequestered Writing

Horses were turned loose in the child's sorrow. Black and roan, cantering
    through snow.
The way light fills the hand with light, November with graves, infancy
    with white.
White. Given lilacs, lilacs disappear. Then low voices rising in walls.
The way they withdrew from the child's body and spoke as if it were
    not there.

What ghost comes to the bedside whispering *You?*
—With its *no one* without its *I*—
A dwarf ghost? A closet of empty clothes?
Ours was a ghost who stole household goods. Nothing anyone would miss.
Supper plates. Apples. Barbed wire behind the house.

At the end of the hall, it sleepwalks into a mirror wearing mother's robe.
A bedsheet lifts from the bed and hovers. Face with no face. *Come here.*
The bookcase knows, and also the darkness of books. Long passages *into,*
Endless histories *toward,* sleeping pages *about.* Why else toss gloves into
    a grave?

A language that once sent ravens through firs. The open world from
    which it came.
Words holding the scent of an asylum fifty years. It is fifty years, then.
The child hears from within: *Come here and know,* below
And unbeknownst to us, what these fields had been.

Blue Hour

for Sean Christophe

The moon slips from its cerement, and my son, already disappearing into
    a man, moves toward his bed for the night, wrapped in a towel of
    lake scent.

A viola, night-voiced, calls into its past but nothing comes.

A woman alone rows across the lake. Her life is intact, but what she
    thought could never be taken has been taken. An iron bridge railing
    one moment its shadow the next.

It is *n'y voir que du bleu,* it is blind to something. Nevertheless.

Even the most broken life can be restored to its moments.

My son rows toward me against the wind. For thirty-six years, he rows.
    In 1986, he is born in Paris.

Bice the clouds, watchet, indigo, woad.

We lived overlooking the cemetery. It was the summer of the Paris
    bombings. I walked him among the graves for what seemed hours but
    were clouds drifting across marble.

Believing it possible to have back the field in its flowering, my friend has
  brought me here, has given me an open window, the preludes, an
  echo of my son's laughter on the rumpled lake.

Go wherever you can but keep returning to the present.

The human soul weighs twenty-six grams. A cathedral can become
  a dovecote.

I was born in America just after the war. My legs grew deformed, and so
  they had to be fitted with a special brace.

At night I banged the brace against the wooden crib bars and cried
  (so they say). The cries had to be stopped before I woke "the
  entire house."

In the morning, footsteps, a wind caught between roofs. From the quarry
  of souls they come into being: supernal lights, concealed light, light
  which has no end.

Everything in the world has a spirit released by its sound.

The room turns white again, and white. For years I have opened my eyes
  and not known where I was.

It was like a kettle wrapped in towels and bubbling, spewing camphor
  clouds against walls turning the world beyond the windows white.

I couldn't move, and when they lifted the tented sheet covering the crib
  it was only to touch my face.

This was the year my mother's mother died in the asylum, Eloise.
  Mindless. Without protection from the world.

Her hair, white, everywhere, her eyes the windows of a ruined house.

Like a kettle, but made of apothecary glass, so that it was possible to
  watch the liquid boil inside.

Sometime later I would find the suitcase of clippings: walls smeared
  with waste, bedsheets mapped in urine, and how later, when Eloise
  burned, they were still tied to their chairs.

By late summer, the fields are high with foamflower, fleabane, loosestrife,
  mullein, and above these wings like chapel windows.

The first love is also there, running through the field as if he could
  escape.

They were in their chairs and in their beds, tied to the bedrails. Some
  had locked themselves in the dispensary, as more than fire they
  feared the world.

Here grow bellflower and blind gentian, blue-eyed grass and touch-me-
  not. I don't know who came into that room but spirits also came.

Objects in the room grew small grew large again. The doll laughed like
    my mother's mother.

In every future window their white gowns, a stone ruin behind a sign
    forbidding trespass for years to come.

They came into the room and left, and later my mother would suffer the
    same emptiness.

In the years just after the war, it was not as certain that a child would
    live to be grown. Trucks delivered ice and poured coal into bins below
    the houses.

You see, one can live without having survived.

———————————

I have returned to Paris: a morning flecked with sparrows, the garret
    casements open over the blue-winged roofs.

The two-storey windows a spackled fresco of sky.

From the *loggia*, it is possible to gaze out over the graves. In the armoire,
    books, and little paper soldiers fighting the Franco-Prussian War.

At the farm-table many afternoons with the windows open, I conjugated
    the *future perfect*, ivy shivering on cemetery walls, the infant asleep—

How is it possible that I am living here, as if a childhood dream had found
    an empty theater in which to mount a small production of its hopes?

———————————

The doors of the coal chutes open. It is the grave of *Svoboda.* A night
    paved with news reports, the sky breaking that the world could be
    otherwise.

One does not forget stones versus tanks. When our very existence broadcast
    an appeal. Shall not say *adieu* when a country ceases to be.

A little later, a burial on a hillside in a pine box.
The empty flesh like stone beneath my hands—

A field lifted into a train window.

Under the ice, hay flowers, anne's lace and lupines. My father digging
    through snow in a fatigue no sleep could relieve.

And the first love, sequestered in an attic room until spring.

———————————

We row to the middle of the lake in a guideboat a century old, water
    pewter in a coming-storm light, a diminishing signature of smoke
    from one of the cabins.

Will his life open to hers, she asks, now that she has traveled all the way
    to the edge of herself?

At night we sleep under blankets also a century old, beside cold stoves
forged at Horseshoe, again a hundred years.

At late day the lake stills, and the hills on the far shore round themselves
in the water.

We climb over rock moss and lichen, through fern stands and up the
rain-slicked trail to the peak.

No longer could she live alone. As if dead, looking into a mirror with
no face.

Star-spangle, woodsia, walking leaf, the ghosts of great blue heron.

What one of us lives through, each must, so that this, of which we are
part, will know itself.

Here, where there was almost nothing, we waited in the birch-lit clouds,
holding the uncertain hand of a lost spirit.

———————

When my son was an infant we woke for his early feeding at *l'heure
bleue*—cerulean, gentian, hyacinth, delft, *jouvence*. What were also
the milk hours.

This one who had come toward me all my life now gazed at the skies
above Montparnasse as if someone were there, gesturing to him from
the slate light.

He looked at me and the asylum shimmered, assembled again into brick-light and wards of madness. Emptiness left my mother. The first love in field upon field.

The dolls were dolls, the curtain a curtain. The one in the grave said yes. *Adieu,* country. *Adieu,* Franco-Prussian War.

Curfew

for Sean

The curfew was as long as anyone could remember
Certainty's tent was pulled from its little stakes
It was better not to speak any language
There was a man cloaked in doves, there was chandelier music
The city, translucent, shattered but did not disappear
Between the no-longer and the still-to-come
The child asked if the bones in the wall
Belonged to the lights in the tunnel
Yes, I said, and the stars nailed shut his heaven

protected from the silence she slid she too
into this loss of self that reaches its height

and is reversed in a clump of charred
roses

—*Jacques Dupin*

Nocturne

What happened? His face was visible then not. Around him snow fell,
    but over him grass remained, wet and young and shaped like a coffin.

I laid her in the snow, she who I was, and walked away.

And the house? Shuttered against fog, awake, windblown.

"The children had cocoa for breakfast, and milk with bread and jam at
    lunch. They took naps in the afternoon. They had a dog. At the end
    of the winter there was 'no more snow.'"

And the cries were those of gulls following a seed plough.

The people of this world are moving into the next, and with them their
    hours and the ink of their ability to make thought.

Particles of light have taken from them *antiphon, asylum, balefire,*
    benediction.

Snow fell onto her coat and chewen gloves, at night like apple blossoms
    in tar, and my solace became that she would remain as she was.

When the house was alive, its walls recorded the rising and falling of the
  bed, as if a wind—

The hurrying-forth took with it *casement, casque, chalice.*

So why does it matter *how,* precisely? Behind a curtain in late day with a
  length of rope. In one of the upper rooms, where a cold rose even
  when the house was shuttered.

His mother on the porch, dressing like a man even then, and the house
  in the photograph behind her in flames, mother and house.

Beneath the ice, open-eyed but absent, she who I was, with ribbon scars
  faint across her. Every tip of wheat-stalk lit by sun.

They took with them *communicant, cruet,* and the ability to keep watch.
  Having lit the night sky, their heaven vanished.

He needed to feel as if he were going to die, many times to feel it, many
  hundreds of times.

It came along and passed beyond. Had I been. Were you not. Because I
  believed I was alone.

Until the derelict house offered its last apparition.

As a star plummets from darkness, a soul is exiled. Light, silk, the rope,
    black storms of dream.

That one day he was given a new mother, and it was she who starved
    them, she who sent them into the wood to cut the very switch—

So with the rope, as if he could replace the past. A child awakened by a
    whip. Until his narrow coffin and cup of sleep.

He was only a boy when the world darkened. But the switches were easy
    to find, so red in winter.

The house where one could dance without clothes imagined an invisible
    piano, stove mice, chimney swallows, a curtain, a cry.

What may have been the beginning of life after death.

In the open arms of a burnt wind he returned to me, barefoot by choice,
    bearing gingerbread, chocolate, quince jam, a bag of candy.

Look! Whole villages intact and shimmering. The very body itself begins
    to evanesce, it has not true boundary. Death changes it as a mirror
    changes a face.

Then he used the past to refer to the present. *Flour-sacks, school-chalk, a
    coherent life.*

Wings slap along the wall, and in the hardened owl dung, crickets glint.
    Dust settles on the house until entire sentences are written.

A window haunted by an open hand. *Here,* he said, his voice like gauze
like grieving.

––––––––––––––––

Over the writing table, an empty map: years to connect the little marks.
In his closet among the linens his weapon of choice.

In answer to your question, no, he could not have done it. The rope was
used for something else, worn from use, a cry a stiffening.

It was with this he untied himself again and again, in the bed and before
the fire, blue-voiced and changed of face.

The house saw everything as does every house. Hollow walls, staircase,
sorrowing ink. It was the last time.

They had been children in towns years apart, she who I was, and the
man in the coroner's arms.

––––––––––––––––

Perhaps those born after the war are those whose lives the war took.

An abandoned house, after all, will soon give itself back, and its walls
become as unreadable as symbols on silk.

With the departed, a sense of time, and sleep even sleep is taken, and the
world appears as if it were—

Every spring I return to her, laying my thoughts to rest like a wreath
on water.

These are the words no longer. Here are the photographs taken when we
were alive.

Refuge

In the blue silo of dawn, in earth-smoke and birch copse,
where the river of hands meets the Elbe.

In the peace of your sleeping face, *Mein Liebchen.*

We have our veiled memory of running from police
dogs through a blossoming orchard, and another

Of not escaping them. That was—ago—(a lifetime),
but now you are invisible in my arms, a soul

Acquiring speech, the body its blind light, whispering
Noli me frangere even as it is in death shattered.

We were *one in the other.* When the doves rose
at once, and our refuge became wing-light—

Writing Kept Hidden

The black fire of ink on paper took hold of their souls—incorporeal fire.

There was no protection this fire couldn't touch nor darkness nor a
moment.

It lasted as long as a dream it was no dream. Heteroglossia of nervous
shortwave, cloud of blown walls.

In the barracks, those who had sketched themselves in coal and smoke
became coal and smoke.

And the living remained, linking unknown things to the known: residue,
scapular, matchlight, name on a tongue.

Then, for an hour, the war slept, and rain filled the cisterns with silence.

Our windows faced east, and on August evenings, the sky was a blue no
longer spoken.

—Beirut, winter 1983

In the Exclusion Zones

Ash over conifers and birches, over berry thickets. Resembling snow and
 its synonyms. Silvered fields of millet.

A silence approaching bees of the invisible or the scent of mint.

One need not go further than a white towel hung in an open door.

Hive

into a light most unexpected the glass hives
executed labors whose writings in a darkness are lost

meanwhile they exhaust the city's supplies
and live only in the midst however abundant

inaudible to them the murmur that comes to us
song of abundance psalms of grief

an entire absence of hesitation
whereby they break with the past as though with an enemy

it is not without prescience their summoning
as though nothing is happening will come back

to live as long as the world itself in those who come after

too vast to be seen too alien to be understood
prefers what is not yet visible to that which is

as a society organizes itself and rises so does a shrinkage enter
so crowded does the too prosperous city become

the era of revolutions may close and work become the barricade
suddenly abandoning generations to come
the abode of the future wrapped in a shroud
a door standing not now where once it stood

we are so made that nothing contents us

Prayer

Begin again among the poorest, moments off, in another time and place.

Belongings gathered in the last hour, visible invisible:

Tin spoon, teacup, tremble of tray, carpet hanging from sorrow's balcony.

Say goodbye to everything. With a wave of your hand, gesture to all you
have known.

Begin with bread torn from bread, beans given to the hungriest, a carcass
of flies.

Take the polished stillness from a locked church, prayer notes left
between stones.

Answer them and hoist in your net voices from the troubled hours.

Sleep only when the least among them sleeps, and then only until the
birds.

Make the flatbed truck your time and place. Make the least daily wage
your value.

Language will rise then like language from the mouth of a still river. No
one's mouth.

Bring night to your imaginings. Bring the darkest passage of your holy
book.

The recollections of a whole life, the consciousness of spiritual existence, and all which is mightiest and deepest in our nature, become brighter, even in opposition to extreme bodily languor. In the immediate vicinity of death, the mind enters on an unaccustomed order of sensations, a region untrodden before, from which few, very few travelers have returned, and from which those few have brought back but vague remembrances; sometimes accompanied with a kind of homesickness for the higher sphere of which they had then some transient prospect. Here, amidst images, dim images, of solemnity or peace, of glory or of terror, the pilgrim pursues his course alone, and is lost to our eye.

—George Burgess, 1850

On Earth

"*now* appears to us in a mysterious light"

"did this happen? could it have happened?"
"everything ahead of her clear for the rest of her life"

"La terre nous aimait un peu je me souviens."

"I try to keep from wanting the morphine. I pray with both hands."

"Lima, Alpha, Uniform, November, Charlie, Hotel, Echo, November,
    Alpha, Bravo, Lima, Echo. Pap. Lima, Charlie, Alpha, Zero, One.
    Acknowledge. Out."

"man and cart disappeared in the blast, but their shadows remained on
    the bridge"

"these diaries a form of weather"

(a future hinting at itself)
(all of this must remain)
(on illness, after radiation; a mysterious illness)
(something) whispering
(the sadness when a hand—)
—with the resistance of a corpse to the hands of the living—

"open the book of what happened"

———————

a barnloft of horse dreams, with basin and bedclothes
a bit of polished quiet from a locked church
a black coat in smoke
a black map of clouds on a lake

a blackened book-leaf, straw and implements
a blue daybook hidden in my bed with his name
a branch weighted with pears

a brittle crack of dawnlight
a broken clock, a boy wakened by his father's whip, then the world as if
        whorled into place —

a broken equation, a partita
a bullet clicking through her hair
a bullet-holed supper plate
a burnt room strewn with toy tanks
a century passing through it

a chaos of microphones
a city a thousand years
a city shaken and snowing

a coin of moonlight on the shattered place
a confusion of birds and fishes
a consciousness not within us
a corpse broken into many countries
a cup of sleep
a desire to live as long as the world itself

a door opening another door
a feather forced through black accordioned paper
a field of birds roasted by the heavens
a goodness that must forget itself
a grave strewn with slipper flowers
a groundskeeper's knowledge of graves

a hole in light, an entrance
a horse grazing in an imaginary field
a horse of wire, wine-corks and wax
a horse tangled in its tether
a hotel haunted by a wedding dress
a house fallen in
a house fallen into itself
a house in time, years from the others, light-roofed, walls shimmering

a hurried life, a knife on newsprint
a lace of recent snow

a language known only to parrots
a life in which nothing is lived
a light, *n'y voir que du bleu,* blind to something
a litany of broken but remembered events

a little hotel in the city with its windows open
a little invention for sweeping crumbs from the table
a locket's parted lovers face to face

a man repainting his wooden house in stopped time
a man vanishing while he danced
a man who built cottages for tourists until he went blind

a memory through which one hasn't lived
a message deflected by other messages
a message from a secret self

a mist of geese rising
a moment of bluesmoke
a moment of sycamores in low mist
a moon caught in the bare hold of firs
a moon haloed in high cirrus

a name which should not be written
a new world, entirely other
a no-longer-beyond

a parcel of copper wire, plastique and a clock
a parrot learning its language from a ghost
a past to come

a phrase shifting epochs
a pinch of salt, a fist of sugar
a plumbago curtain withdrawn from the radiance
a poplar in the sun, a pouch of coins, between layers of sleep where one
    lives another life beside this, awakening in the grave, brushing
        mother's hair in the kitchen

a random life caught in a net of purpose
a record-keeper of human and earthly life

a rifle loaded with moments
a rivulet of sweat on the brow of the one keeping watch

a road erased by light
a road that ends nothing

a salvage yard of burnt office furniture and household goods
a scarf of smoke from a mouth
a schooner sailing in a bottle of light

a scriptorium

a search without hope for hope
a searchlight washing the fields
a secret that stands apart from every secret

a single turn, then years on the same road
a snow of ash risen from winter months

a spiral of being
a spirit gold-breathed, something not made only of
a stairwell spiraling
a stalled ambulance

a steep wooden staircase
a sudden reticence that seizes the heart
a syllable a dove

a taxi and three gunmen
a taxi its four doors open its lights out
a telephone ringing in an empty house
a ticking telex
a traffic jam of refugees on a desert road

a train rounding low sand hills

a veiled window a camera hidden in a loaf of bread
a veiled window where appears a revenant
a walnut box of world and light
a war-eyed woman

a web of survivals
a wind of burnt documents borne by wind
a white rain, then your face becoming another's
a white road
a white road billowing behind the relief trucks
a white road ending in one's own life

a whitened eye clouded with gnats
a willow vase, more bedsheets flaring over the furniture
a wind lifting washed linen

a wind-flock of butterflies
a window of grilled hens
a wire fence woven with pine boughs

a woman in a blowing coat on the tarmac
a woman rubbing the mirror until she is gone
a woman sitting on a window ledge as if about to vanish

a word dissolved into the yet-again
a world set in language and deserted
a world thought into being

a wreath on water
a year passing through itself
a yellow mosaic of remains

above a pacific slumber of white houses
above a *salon de thé*
absent in a garden of watered roses
acres of blue wind

after having gone all the way to the end
after his internment and before his suicide
again and again
against a sea of recriminations
against a winter pine, eating a sparrow
against this, that

air filled with ash, notebooks with sorrowing ink
airfield to airfield
algebraic music
all night the boats calling out
all of them, *à-dieu*
all questioning to myself

allées of tall trees
alluvial plains
alpha rays of plutonium

although we are a small group on a private tour
America a warship on the horizon at morning

American university T-shirts among the executed
among white birch stands
an ache of such light
an ache of such light fixed in the bone
an anonymous work performed
an authorized death a non-authorized death

an inn for phantoms

an inner tact
an object that disappears from the word
an olive field of ordnance
an ossuary
an oven of birds

ancient light having reached us
and all questions, and all questions about questions
and among the stars, those too distant to be seen
and collective memory a dread of things to come
and for women who desire men
and have left undone

and in the dream *Ce voyage, je voulais le refaire*
and in the villages laundry hanging for months
and in their eyes the years taken from them
and it is certain someone will be at that very moment pouring milk

and it is supposed that we are describing the world
and its corresponding moment in the past
and night, a knock at the window
and night, a storehouse

and on the battlefield, our anatomy lessons
and phrases like: vanishing pianos
and she body and promising light she exists
and silence the most mysterious form of affection

and standing in phosphorus rain, the man I have not yet married
and that another will be uttering its first human word

and the glass-winged bats hang in the darkness
and the gun though loud has not discharged
and the house? there. which became what it was because of us

and the marigold the flower of worry
and the shell etching a horizon into our window as it passed
and the trains, the way they come, they tell me it is not the truth but I
    remember it
and time, speeding as it departs
and we fell into each other laughing the laugh of the newly dead

and we, separated on earth by decades
and what intervened more, war or the passage of time?
and what of those who have made this same journey?

and whispering what could
and *writing*, the guardian of the past

angelica, anne's lace, antiphon, aria, ash, asylum
another child filling its mouth with pillow
ants in a city of peony
apparition in a vacant house
appears to feel the soul go forth

apple blossoms and wet wind
approaching the other with empty hands

aria in time of war
armfuls of furze, lupine, cornflower

as a flame is linked to its burning coal
as a mirror changes a face
as a rain, however brief, changes the world
as all afternoon the clouds float west to east, leaf-smoke and lake wind,
    pumice and plumbago gray, white-storeyed, rain-logged

as any backward look is fictive
as any conflagration or struggle is understood
as any new act inflicts its repetition
as crows mark the fog

as for children, so for the dead
as gloves into a grave
as God withdrawing so as to open an absence

as he appears and reappears in the unknown
as if a flock of geese were following
as if there were no other source of food
as if to say goodbye to his own mind
as if we had only one more hour

as if with the future we could replace the past
as in the childhood of terror and holiness
as light or the retreat of light

as memory, a futile attempt
as more beautiful than it had been because it is lost

as rain before it reaches us
as rain strikes the pails in our tents of wakefulness
as the fence has recorded the wind
as the water in which the corpse has been washed
as those who have returned have said

as though when past and present converge, there is a gap
as thought affects the universe in as yet immeasurable ways
as unexpected rain craters the fields
as when cicadas sing at the cenotaph

ascending to the stone-cool stars
ash manuscript, death aria, hunger fugue
ash sailing ashen wind

at once in this world and the world to come
at the city's edge the aged cooling towers
at the edge of a forest once for making violins
at the end of their journey, the petals they carry vanish
at the end, where they carry his body
at the point where language stops

at the ticket window, and again in the fruit stalls, a kilo of open melon, in
    the train without stopping, rain of yellow tickets, broken turnstile
at writing's border, as if memory were of everyone, forgetting no one,
    such a cold happiness!

awakening *dans le vrai*

back to the blowing-out of birthday candles
back to the crystal ring of a toast
back to the furl of his shirt in a hot wind
back to the razing of every edifice
balefire, balcony, balm, belief, benediction

bamboos bleached by light
bananas hacked clean on the stalk, tangerines pulled down with their leaves
bare trees in fog, umbrellas opening all at once
barefoot by choice in the thin sea, by choice wearing black cotton

bats hanging from the rafters, long polished corridors open
bats singing along walls
because we cannot emerge

beds in the great open-air sickbay
before and behind us
behind the face that speaks to us and to whom we speak
beings who have chosen one another
bell music rolling down the roofs

between here and here
between hidden points in the soul
between hidden points in the soul born from nothing
between saying and said
beyond what one has oneself done

birchbark curling from the birch limbs
birds dropping from flight leaving cries in the air
birds in the clerestory, a tapestry of broken light

biting hard the fear
black corn in the fields, crib smoke, and bones enough to fill a sack
black fingernails, blue hands, lost hair
black storms of dream
black with burnt-up meaning

blessed be *a knowledge that burns thought*
blood rose and love
blossoming poplars
blossoming walls, a grave digger's tunic, a newspaper kiosk in rain
blossoms yet again inside us

blue lobelia rising along the gate
blue-leaved lilies
blue-winged roofs and rooflight
boat scraps washed leeward

bone child in the palm a bird in the heart
bone-clicking applause of the winter trees
bones of the unknown
bones smoothed by water
book of smoke, black soup
born with a map of calamity in her palm

both windows open to whatever may happen
bottled light tossed into the sea with no message

bring forth what is within
bring in your whispering harvest

broken clouds return from the past
broken space, ruined birds, death's heaven

but in a change of worlds you weren't you
by someone who *was not* and would not *revient*
by the time we were face to face
by which *we* is not the plural of *I*
Ça ne veut pas rien dire

caged canaries before each shop as if the street were a mineshaft
canticle, casement, casque, cerement, cinder

capable of a fate other than its own
cathedral bells chiseling the winter air
cathedral of shivering light
Ce voyage, je voulais le refaire

certain of thought but not of what is seen
chandeliers in shellfire, chaotic light

charnel house of the innocents
checkpoints, roadblocks, barricades, points of entry
children shouting goodbye in a hot wind
christmas lights in smoke
cinema does not describe this moment

city through the filth of a bus window
clouds of lake water, light and speech
clouds of road behind us
clouds returning to the sky from the past

cocoa, whistling pine, ceiba, ylang-ylang, rain
code for key turns
cognac steadying the night

cold fire-pit
cold stalks of daylily
come, love, through burning
composed of light
converging on my own life

cordite wind, one's first cordite
corn black in the fields, crib smoke, bones, a rib cage
corrugated fields, sheep on the bare fields of drought
cotton mats spread on the floors of classrooms
countries erased from their maps

cratered memory cratered field
crows took rye scraps from her hands
curtains of rain opening

dark, borne within us
dead woman giving birth to rats
dear Françoise of bravery under fire
death is not the conclusion of earthly life
death is the descent of the one called

décryptage
destroys what it briefly illuminates
detritus reaching through a window washed away by wind

difference which she is not to speak
digging a hole in the floor for no apparent reason

disquiet and the book of disquiet
dissolved into the yet-again
distance measured in space or time
do we *interpret* the words before we obey the order?

doors opening, stones humming the foretold
dovecote, drum, dust
doves on the gray limbs of winter poplar

down a desert road aerially strafed
drawings doomed to be destroyed by bullets
dreaming nouns remembered until a window
dressed in their shrouds
drinking from cupped hands
dwelling in apartness

each a ring of soot
each day breaking along the cordillera, then broken
each page a window intact until touched

early summer's green plums
earth singing in her magma chambers
easter lilies opening in

elegiac time
empty windows dipped in milk
enigma, escritoire, estuary
enough seen. enough had. enough

even if by forgetting
even if he is thousands of miles away or dead
even the trembling of souls turning into light

every line in his face the river of a single year
except to be gentle with one who loved you mistakenly and very much
expectation, the presence of the not-yet-exiled from itself

filled with lifelong gratitude
fire of human becoming
fired from the tip of the only possible
fireflies above the graves, time collapsing, your name which should not
    have been in stone in stone

firing into the air five nights in the shelter
firmament, fissure, flare stars, frottage

flags opening in wind
flatbread like a stack of plates on his arm
flocks of geese marching in formation down a dust road
flowering trees: trumpet, bottlebrush, cassia, frangipani, flame, sea grape
flowers rotting on mounds: air plant, allamanda, amaryllis, spider lily,
        bougainvillea, shellflower, hibiscus, ashanti blood, trumpet
          vines, oleander

for the rest of your life, search for them
for the words that would not come

forward to a rope from his arm to the post
forward to a wedding-cake knife in our hands
forward to the blindfold
forward to the list of demands
fountains of dust rising out of the hills

fragments from the Second Brandenburg
fresh wind in the linens
from a gloved hand a flaming bottle
from chance to chance, event to event
from earth to satellite, event to event
from our last train ride through the ricefields
from the cathedral comes *Kyrie*

garbage fires along the picket lines
gasoline coupons and rations, an event no longer remote
Georg leaning against the winter pine eating a sparrow
ghost hands appearing in windows, rubbing them clear
ghost swift, grisaille, guardian spirit

God not a being but a force, and humans, the probative tip of that
          becoming
God withdrawn from the world

gourds, relief sacks loaded into trucks, poles, rags, tents
graves marked with scrap iron, a world in her dead eye
grief of leave-taking
ground fog rising from a graveyard

had gathered to die
> *had it changed?*

had undergone subtle and perilous shiftings

half-tracks and yellow-eyed transports, and behind them a long road
happens when you say yes
happiness without fulfillment

having made herself stand she was at rest
hayloft, hillock, hoarfrost, hush

he is from exile, which is in all of them
he listened to Schubert, *Tosca*
he saw nothing of what was to come
he told her how, in those years
he, though alive, was no longer

her amnesia an approach to understanding her life

her face the war years
her hair a banner of rain
her hands blue in the well
her wet skirt wrapping her legs

hills thinning at the world's edge
his absence fills with passing clouds, the script of birds, and
    schoolchildren's voices
his ashen hands having passed through the window of his truck
his can of dark tobacco, his yellow finch in a cage
his footsteps disappearing as he walked
his grave strewn with slipper flowers and sardine cans

his hands, detritus reaching through a window washed away
his words sparkling in the raw air

history branded with the mark of uncertainty
history decaying
history decaying into images

horse clearing an obstacle
horses, poppies, trees with trunks like sycamores and leaves like maples
hot, the hurry of stars
hour of no matins
house of being

how abandoned how left behind
how better to account for my life
how did this happen? how it always happens.
how it reads its past

how secretly you died for years, on behalf of all who wished for themselves
    a private death
how the soul becomes an inhabitant of flesh

I am alone, so there are four of us
I am here, blowing into my hands, you are in the other coffin
I can't possibly get away, she said

I lit a taper in the Cathédrale St-Just, a two-franc candle, birds flying in
    the dome
I remember standing next to his bed
I see myself in their brass coat-buttons but not in their eyes

I stand on the commode for a glimpse of it

I tried once. it was just before the war, and she had no time for me. *I can't possibly get away*

I was to bring him music for the left hand

idam agnaye, na mama

idam agnaye, na mama (this is for the fire, not for me)

if he exists to another, that is need

if rope were writing he would have hanged himself

if you ask him what happened he will tell you

if you bring forth what is within you

in a bowl polished by the morning light

in a village where the women know how to piss standing up

in carceral silence

in glimpses, broken messages, cryptic signs

in his address book, a pressed poppy chosen from his mother's poppy bed

in his coat, a small cage of canaries

in his hand a clod of himself to wipe on the walls

in memory: the music of an open spigot

in reverse until you were floating in a flat green boat

in solitary reverie we can tell ourselves everything

in stone is written *in stone*

in the bardo of becoming

in the black daybreak, passing through

in the casket window, a face

in the cellar, three crates: rifles, gold & cognac
in the cesium fields
in the chaotic light in the coal-smoked heavens
in the cities of what can be said
in the country of advanced years
in the ecstasy of standing outside oneself
in the fact of parting

in the garden: heliotrope, phlox, rose trees, trellised roses, blue torenia,
    hibiscus, blue lobelia, lichen, a bamboo grove
in the garden in winter with my son

in the mathematical language of a time to come
in the morning, a white shirt on the line waving
in the night photograph: electric cities, burning forests
in the pole-and-rag tents

in the still-bandaged pines
in the summer, weeds took over the city: horse weeds known as railway
    weeds grew taller than people

in the surround of that word
in the time after
in the tin lamp's punched light

in the toy store, a parcel of toys explodes
in the white infinity of mist
in the window a veil of winter
in their radiance a tub of dry milk
in this camp, how many refugees
in this the child's blue hour

in thought, where they were lost
incapable of imagining annihilation
inhabiting a body to be abolished

inter alia, inter nos
intercessor

into a duration deep within her
into the world, further illuminated by thought

iris, illuminant

is there anything else?
it appears to be an elegy, put into the mouth of a corpse

it became what it was because of us—in that sense *loved*
it is as if space were touching itself through us
it is more ominous than any oblivion, to see the world as it is

it is not possible to find you in death's heaven
it is not raining in the catacombs
it is not you who will speak
it is the *during* of the world
it is the morning of the body's empty soul

it is worse than memory
it ruins time, the chiasmus of hope

it was all over
it was all there, written in stone, a record of munitions
it was *cinema*

it was gruel refused: blue wedges of bread, maggot soup, rice drippings
it was just before the second war, and she had no time for me
it was raining in the catacombs
it was the first time in my life I tasted fish

it was the name of a time, and over there, a place
it was the simplest way to know one another
J'ai rêvé tellement fort de toi
J'ai tellement marché tellement parlé

journey of two thousand kilometers
journey that will have no end
keeping a record of oneself
keepsake, knell, Kyrie

knowing oneself from within
l'heure bleue, hour of doorsteps lit by milk

le musée hypothétique

lace patterned after frost flowers
language from chance to chance

languid at the edge of the sea
lays itself open to immensity
leaf-cutter ants bearing yellow trumpet flowers along the road
left everything left all usual worlds behind
library, lilac, linens, litany

lifting the wounded

light and the reverse of light
light impaled on the peaks
light issuing from the wind's open wounds
light mottling the forest floor, crows leaving one limb for another
light of cinder blocks, meal trays
light of inexhaustible light

lighted paper sacks sent downriver to console
like the handkerchief road
like the whispering in a convent garden
like tomb flowers, the ossuary's skull works
lilac and globeflower, clouds islanding the tilled fields

linked as flame to burning coal, as one candle lighted from another
listening to the stove mice and chimney swallows
little rain holes where the bullets went, rains crater the field, raising
    each a ring of soot, striking the catch pails and stabbing the tarpaulin.
    we live in fog tents, awake, whispering what could once be written
        on a sliver of rice

lost in paper, shellfire
lupine wind, lingering daylight
lute music written for severed hands

manuscripts in the cold part of the house
matchbooks flaring in a blank window
matinal, mirage, mosaic
meaning did not survive that loss of sequence

memory does not interfere
memory the presence of the no-more

metal soup pots hung to dry, crazed porcelain basins
mirrors, vials, furnaces
misprision of moments lifted from their concealment
moments of rain ascend in the manner of smoke

more ominous than any oblivion
mortar smoke mistaken for an orchard of flowering pears

mud from the bowels of the city
mud from the disheveled night
music loosening floor tiles, a moon washed in earthly light, the dawn
    sirens calling men to the mines
music of the hurrying fountains
must release the dead from bondage
must rise from the dead while we live

my dear, I think *yes*
my father crossed the field and stood
my hair a cold flag of rain
my hands coated with tomb dust
my mother's hand broken by a fierce wind
my own: I was utterly there. and when I came back I was still there
naked beneath our names, thrown up by the wit-lost
near dawn, near the river wasn't it? if one of us

near the lake, where the fireweed was
neither a soul nor a body

neither for us nor near itself
never repeating itself
nevertheless, noumenon, november

new pasts, whole aeons are invented

night shift in the home for convalescents
nightshirt, razor strop, boot-heel
night-voiced viola

no breath of God, no words, and no possibility of restoration
no content may be secured from them
no one prayer resembling another

not a house but a stagnant hour
not blood, flesh and bread but an earthly ecstasy
not isolation but a lack of solitude
not only the flow of thoughts, but their arrest
not wishing to know anything more about oneself

nothing as it was
nothing other than mind
nothing was exiled from itself
now and again like a voice grown suddenly tired

now on the plane in a white-out
objects [heavenly bodies] *as they were in the past*
oder nicht

oil soap, orchard, ossuary
old books snowing from our hands

older than clocks and porcelain, younger than rope
older than glass, younger than music
on each tip of grass a wet jewel
on her hand, a moment of ring-light

on lave les corps, on les prépare pour l'ensevelissement
on the blanket then, government issue

on the fifty-fourth day, loss of sight and hearing
on the platform between trains, holding a bottle
on the shortwave, the high whine of the world's signal

one for the other
one sees and is seen
one sees and is seen approaching the other with empty hands
one stands in line for butter
only the walls that did not face the blast remained white
open shell of heaven

or a failed letter
or that she would admonish me for the years of my silence
or when it first occurred to them to have graves with markers

our atelier of passing trains, citronella smoke, a veiled bed
our hymnic song against death
our most secret selves

past and present sliding into each other
pear trees espaliered along the walls
pen and ink across the boundaries
pink snow downwind of the test site

pinning their intentions to a saint's dress
pitch smoke chalks the sky over the roof
poppy seed, portal, portrait, prayerbook

present though most often invisible
question after question
quiescent, quiet, quinine, quivering

rain falling into their open eyes
rain in the catacombs
raising each a ring of soot

redemption not an accounting or a debt
refugee, relic, reverie
relief sacks loaded into trucks
relief tents until the horizon
remaining in fear of death but remaining
responsible beyond our intentions

resting language or language under surveillance
reverses itself as we read it

riddles the statues of martyrs and turns
rinses limbs then craters the field
rinses limbs then
rises as wet smoke
rising in bodily light
roads rivered with waste and a tea-colored rain
sacks of soy and manioc, dry milk, rice
sanctuary, sea glass, sorrow
scoop of earth: slivers of femur, metacarpals

searching for something one knows will not be found
set in language and deserted by God

she heard no one's footsteps, then nothing
she holds lilacs to her face
she meets a man on the mule-steps who has been dead for months
she pulled the lilacs to herself
she puts the rice pot down in the snow
she sees nothing of what is to come

she went with him willingly and without knowing where she was, she
    saw the country very much as she would have had she walked
    through a film about herself
she within me
she would never again wander too far into the past

sheltering in the open
shore birds, smoke, the ferris wheel turning
signature by signature in triplicate, rice and dry milk
since last night on the bridge
six hours under fire along the road
six inches from my belly
sixteen clicks after the flag of fire

slow questioners, there was no place in the world for them

smacking the hands of children who miswrote
small talk like white smoke from kindling
snow clicking as it falls into itself, hushed, a little smoke crawling from a
    stovepipe, following the wind or rising straight, the village so quiet
        that one can hear the iced branches

snow in the shadow folds, *impasto, gouache*
snow on the shoulders of the statuary
so as not to take a single word into my mouth
so as to be taken for refugees
so emptiness cannot harm emptiness
so it appears as if it were what we wanted

so that the dead climb up out of the river to blacken its banks
so that the other comes back

so this is how the past begins—
so we walked, pretending our empty suitcases burdened us
some dance, one holds a dove aloft
some flaw in the message itself
some were burned with cigarettes, some doused with turpentine. every
    night they poured turpentine through their hair and slept like that,
    so as to keep the leeches from giving them head wounds

some with wicker baskets, others with gathered flax, some with children
    in their arms, others with brooms, some dance, others hold aloft a dove
someone will be pouring milk while another perishes

something broken and personal, a memory
something holding back the pouring, a turn of the kaleidoscope, a turn
    again, radiant, beautiful, meaningless so it is easier to choose stones
    from the ground, a sack of words, pieces of language from something
    larger, and if a single event caused this ruin, what was that event?
        what made night a country of terror?

something within me is no longer with him
snow catching on razor wire, searchlit fields

snow through open windows
soul on its way toward earth
sparks of holiness
spoken in unknown words of a known language

stepping back into an earlier life
strands of hair, blood, corpuscled light
streets iced with shop-glass, a flock of stones
stripped trees against winter fields

take no words by mouth
tangled lilacs, peeling walls, darkening lindens
tedium taught me an imaginary world
tendril, torpor, tributary

that even this refuge might be taken:
that ing-ing of verbs in an eternal present
that light traveled from the eye to the world
that nothingness might not be there
that you might become one among others
the after-touching memory of relief

the air around the ringing bells filled with ash
the being that lies half open

the birds became smoke
the blue whorling that once spoke
the blue-stoned streets of river rock
the boiling, sudden clouds of August

the border. anywhere. but the war zone. mattresses roped to the roof
the boundless etcetera of indifference

the breath of the invisible
the bridge that doesn't touch the other bank
the buildings of the center city no longer

the candlelit stairwells in blackout
the cedared hills, smoking orchards, and the rivers of ill luck

the cemetery workman's wheelbarrow
the chandelier of water against stone
the chorus of mules and roosters, goat bells, little cries
the cinema, trip-wired, the small-arms fire

the click, night
the click, night, pages turned by a wind and taken
the confessions written in gunpowder and spit
the danger of premature good conscience
the dawn sky at morning pearl and smoke, the trees stripped

the day has not yet come
the day will of all days be ordinary, its weather various

the dead were left among the living—there were no questions
the dead were washed and dressed and touched
the *densissimus imber* of the rain

the dreams are a coffin with an open window
the dreams of a mind in the grave

the early summer's green plums
the empty wet shirts on the line waving
the endless, unbroken lines
the evacuation of ghosts

the flautist's breath in a stairwell
the flumes of white phosphorus marking the city
the *for* and *for*
the forbidden world hidden behind it

the four-a.m. bombing of a newspaper office
the fragility of social orders
the furthest edge
the future destroying us

the ganglia of a train map, metastasizing cities
the going-forth, the as-yet-cannot-be-heard
the greater and lesser wings
the ground luminosity

the hand moving of its own accord across the page
the happy life life itself
the hidden world and its inhabitants
the hole of my mouth
the hole where my ancestor stands burning

the house, a white portrait of our having fled
the hushed chill of such a wind
the *I*'s time, in which things happen
the ice of reminiscence submerged in time

the immigrant disappearing into a new language
the informant's diary of his whereabouts

the ivory of ice on the rivers
the japonica's shadow on a telegraph pole
the life that would have ended then goes on

the light in these old photographs is a palm of rice
the light of a pocket mirror moving through trees

the little notebook of poems in the pocket of a corpse
the Lumière camera
the man tipping his hat sadly
the man tipping his hat sadly as if to say goodbye to his own mind

the mirror in her eyes giving himself back
the moon a bone-cap of ice or ivory
the moon in its clearing
the morning's cold light on the blankets
the mortar smoke mistaken for an orchard of flowering pears

the name I am becoming
the nine lights of thought
the open well ending in its moon of water
the opening of time

the past is white near the sea
the past, which is our present
the peace of a black-windowed warehouse
the peace of the hay

the *pleroma* which she did not desire for herself
the plummet of a star from its darkness
the question speaks *the very language of lack*

the rain falls lightly now
the rescuers lift from the wreckage a child no longer a child
the revenant whispers: *forgive me if I am wrong but I could not sleep*

the roads issuing mist
the roads rivered with sewage and tea-colored rain
the roofs have fallen, field flowers grow in the rooms. nevermind

the same clicking of bare limbs in wind
the same rose sold to every mourner
the secret police having risen to the stature of petty thieves
the sedimentary years
the shacks of *le quartier de la guerre*

the silence of a new language
the soft houses of heaven
the soldiers' moonlit helmets

the soul cannot leave the body of a suicide until she comes
the soul weighs twenty-six grams and is migratory like the birds
the soul, enamored of greatness
the soul with its sense of destination, the soul exiled, a stranger to earth

the space between events infinite
the stench of soap boiling at the edge of a village
the sting of bleached linen

the stony space where all of this happens
the stories nested, each opening to the next
the story of empty rice sacks
the street's memory of abandoned shoes
the streets running with a sweet gray stench

the sun a monstrance
the sun moving toward *Lambda Herculis*
the sun will turn into a red giant, and then into a white dwarf
the sweet stench of gangrene, a cloud of flies, in its hand a child's
    necropolis

the temptation of temptation
the three hidden lights beyond the grasp of thought

the tomb into which we escape

the trains. sometimes a silent coupling
the trees: almond, annatto, sweetsop, banana, monkey-bread, bay rum,
    sandal bead, breadfruit, yellowsilk, camphor, candle
the trees mortared into flower
the trembling of river stones, the ignition of spirit, the firing of human
    thought
the trip wire in white grass at one with the footfall, the latch

the truck-rutted fields the burnt sorrow
the twenty-two bones of the skull
the uncertain hand of a lost spirit
the vanished present visible on earth

the wall of white sand and poisonous mill wastes
the way one could bathe while still covered by a square of cloth
the wet paper of flesh draped on brittle bone

the what is? gives the wrong answer
the what is? has ruined thought

the white train
the white-boned noon

the window covered with a wool blanket
the woman in the flowered robe mad with fear
the woman in your arms a lighted bedcloth
the world an accident
the world as it emerges
the world's ensouling in a gallery of sadness

their bedclothes soaked in music
their bruises, aubergine
their refusal to accompany us further

their souls exist as their body
their souls shuttered against hope
then at dawn through the cedars
then for an hour we slip photographs from their frames, strip the walls,
     toss what had been our life into shipping crates
then phosphorus fell silver on the city and rained on the lettuce fields

there is a reason you have lost him. for the rest of your life you could
     search for it

there is no absence that cannot be replaced
there is no reason for the world
there was black corn in the fields, crib smoke, and bones enough to fill
    the sack
there was no *when* there
there was nothing that wasn't for sale

these are my contents
these paving stones this hymnal
these ruins are to the future what the past is to us

they bind them in rags
they climb out of the river and blacken its banks
they died along with anyone who knew who they were
they fell from heaven to earth

they go on past grief and give me a sack of beans
they lived in the carcass of the sports coliseum
they looked into the camera, into the future

they will gladly go to the precipice, but where is the precipice?
thinking *against* the world
this end and the beginning within it
this is a *musée hypothétique*:
this is a transit camp, a squatters' camp
this is how things were for us then
this is the city. this is a photograph of the city

this is the city. this was the city
this only death can write
this open-air asylum

this ossuary of world, what is the phrase for it?
this reversal
this shattering of indifference
this sudden incipience of event—

those things are obvious which are invisible
those who have entered and have left unharmed
thoughts turned back into ink and paper
throwing light upon light

time—"a severe border guard"—becomes imaginary
time lapsed in one country is only beginning in another
time, to which we are exiled

to abandon yearning for the body
to be unquiet
to be visible to oneself
to become endlessly what one has been
to cross the field without breaking the snow
to enter into itself and to stay awake
to expose ourselves to whatever may happen
to forget once having known it
to hide, safeguard, entrust to a protected place

to know not only what is, but the other of what is
to know that the great bell is the great bell

to remain haunted
to rescue the future
to say nothing without confining ourselves to silence
to search like a sheep for salt

to see or to perish
to see other than from without
to see the world as it actually is

to walk the quays among the executed
to where a drawn lamb is hanging beheaded

today the world is stiff and locked in place, pines still, skies droning,
    snow mounded, and everyone has gone "to work"

together into the blue but unbroken perishing

too many bones in too small a soul
torn curtain, shutters in wind
toward what end? what uniformity?

tunneling between worlds
twirling organdy dresses waving goodbye
two children in his arms
two discontinuous realms

un enfant qui meurt, wrapped in a trouser leg
under the blind sky's surveillance
under the whip, invisible, in the not-there
under what conditions can we speak of
une enfant qui meurt wrapped in a trouser leg
unspeakable in language
unspoken thoughts, leaving us in their proximity, alone
until dawn in the fire tower
until this, that

vesture, vigil light, votive
visible only to God

walking the streets, tented in bedclothes
war-eyed in the warehouse of history
war *no longer declared but only continued*
warning us of its nature and our own
washing its windows until they vanish

was this not to know me?

watch them appear to recede: what are we seeing?
water calm to the wind line
water rosy with iron
waters filled with human belief
watery cathedral, a gold wash of light, a trembling—

we are as paper against the walls of the passage
we caused each other
we drove through disappearing villages
we hid among tangerine peels, lamb bones and blue figs
we lived in tents of fog
we returned to the border and walked toward the checkpoint

we take our *citron pressé*, your hand mine, and the clocks spin in reverse
    until you are floating in a flat green boat
we take our worldly goods, your hand, mine, and the clocks spin

we were spoken into being
were we not?

wet bouquets at the kiosk
wet paper of our flesh

what crawled out of the autumn wood was dementia
what did we retrieve? empty spectacles?
what do these questions ask?

what do we have to forget?
what end? what uniformity?
what fragmentary light?

what God does or does not forgive
what is closest to us
what is it? must be answered *who is it?*
what sees us without being seen
what waking life is to the dream
what was before, imperfectly erased
what were we doing as far away as this?
what you see is the beginning of life after death
what you see you shall become
when did we know?
when I opened the door
when it was possible to walk across the river
when one could hear, behind the curtain, the whole thing
when the thing had gone beyond the limits of a room
when this sunlight reaches the future
when time seems to us a *queer thing*
when we wake from our deaths

when you know the worst, you can return to cut stalks of iris in April
where at least one loveliness wanders
where else would they have fallen?
where everything destroyed was left intact
where he looked
where the helicopters landed, lifting trees from the ground
where the ore is crushed into yellowcake
where the sickness knew us

where there is some message to convey
where they go without sleep
where thinking takes place we have a right to say
while I lived in that other world, years went by in this one

while out on the cobalt sea the ship turns toward us
while we watched transfixed the repetitive novelty of death

who cries for the jasmin as he digs them up, and carries with him a can
    of black tobacco and a yellow finch in a cage
who if rope were writing would have hung himself
who in mirrors saw a strange woman
who no longer realized I was there
who returns from the journey with her eyes ruined
who wanted only to retrieve a few invisible souvenirs:
who wrote on the window in lipstick *I will never forget you*
whose white hands lift from this river the sudden flight of cranes

why do I seem no longer alive?
wide-planed wind of the sea
wild doves in a warehouse
willow, windthrow, winter, wisteria

wind etching the walls
wind singing in the chimney
windows X'd against fire

windshield wipers clearing a wedge of water
wisteria floating along the fence

with a camera hidden in a loaf of bread
with empty suitcases, pretending to be refugees
with how much uncertainty they told it

with revolutionary hope we searched, believing
with the flurry of a dovecote
without passing through thought
without personal history or desire for selfhood
without so much as a biscuit tin of water

without wandering too far into the past
woman in black holding daisies in paper
woman in mourning black with baskets of lemons and eggs
wood crates of cognac and ordnance

wooden crosses in snow
words burning in the windows
words carried by countless mouths
work shoes, soda cans, holy braided palm
world without having been
world without origin

would return to the point of departure
would reveal itself as other than chance

writing, an anguished wind
written over an open grave

x does not equal

yet the women dancing with white scarves
yet the women veiled in cirrus

you are the ghost through whom we see the wall
you come to earth in your sorrows
you, leaping tall fields, cornflower and milk
you might be the revenant of the earliest years, you might be within
you must leave, you cannot remain here, you must leave at once

you spit out your teeth, give it up
you will see the generation into which you should have been born

your churches will warehouse weapons and wheat
your freedom is an abyss

your hand awkward between us in the absence of love
your heart in the guise of mysterious words
your light narrow coffin
your mother waving goodbye in the flames
your notebooks, the sorrow of ink

your things have been taken
your things have been taken away

zero

May 2001

Afterdeath

from the quarry of souls they come into being
supernal lights, concealed light, that which has no end

that which thought cannot attain
the going-forth, the *as yet cannot be heard*

—as a flame is linked to its burning coal
to know not only what is, but the other of what is

Notes

"Blue Hour" When my son was an infant in Paris, we woke together in the light the French call *l'heure bleue*, between darkness and day, between the night of a soul and its redemption, an hour associated with pure hovering. In Kabbalah, blue is *hokhmah*, the color of the second *sefirah*. In Tibetan Buddhism, the hour before dawn is associated with the ground luminosity, or "clear light," arising at the moment of death. It is not a light apprehended through the senses, but is said to be the radiance of mind's true nature.

Everything in the world has a spirit released by its sound.
—John Cage to Oskar Fischinger, 1984

"In the Exclusion Zones" refers to the thirty-kilometer radius of contaminated lands immediately surrounding the Chernobyl nuclear reactor.

"Hive" is after Maurice Maeterlinck.

"On Earth" was written during the spring of 2001.

Gnostic abecedarian hymns date from the third century A.D. Along with Christian and Buddhist texts, they were recovered from small towns on the northern fringe of the Taklamakan Desert early in the twentieth century. The texts were written in seventeen languages, including Sogdian and Tocharian, as well as Aramaic and the "Estrangelo script," a script for Syriac.

appears to feel the soul go forth

—Lucretius, *De rerum natura* (translated by W. H. Mallock)

a knowledge that burns thought

—Maurice Blanchot

I am alone, so there are four of us

—Gaston Bachelard

La terre nous aimait un peu je me souviens

—René Char

behind the face that speaks to us and to whom we speak

—Emmanuel Levinas

black with burnt-up meaning

—Julia Kristeva

Ça ne veut pas rien dire: this does not mean nothing
Ce voyage, je voulais le refaire: this journey I wanted to make again
dans le vrai: in the midst of things

enough seen. enough had. enough

—Arthur Rimbaud

idam agnaye, na mama: this is for the fire, not for us.

—Vedic mantra

Il n' y a pas d'absence irremplaçable: there is no absence that cannot be replaced

—René Char

J'ai rêvé tellement fort de toi / J'ai tellement marché tellement parlé: I have dreamed so strongly of you / I have walked so much, talked so much

—attributed to Robert Desnos

not only the flow of thoughts, but their arrest

—Walter Benjamin

oder nicht: or not

on lave les corps, on les prépare pour l'ensevelissement: one washes the bodies,
one prepares them for burial

pleroma: fullness, plenitude; in Gnostic theology, the spiritual universe as the
abode of God and of the totality of the divine powers and
emanations

musée hypothétique: hypothetical museum

—after the painter Ashley Ashford-Brown, of Ivry-sur-Seine

the very language of lack

— Edmond Jabès

une enfant qui meurt: a child who dies

zero: also the "pure zero" of C. S. Peirce's semiotic metaphysics

With gratitude to my editor, Terry Karten; my literary agent, Virginia Barber;
the poets Frank Bidart, Robert Creeley, Barbara Cully, Forrest Gander, Louise
Glück, Lise Goett, Ellen Hinsey, Fanny Howe, Ilya Kaminsky, Semezdin
Mehmedinović, Honor Moore, Michael Palmer, Robert Pinsky, Lloyd
Schwartz, C. D. Wright; and, as ever, my friend Svetozar Daniel Simko and
my dear husband, Harry Mattison, for readings of this work during its
making.

About the Author

Carolyn Forché is the author of *Gathering the Tribes*, winner of the Yale Younger Poets Award, which received awards from the Academy of American Poets and the Poetry Society of America, and *The Angel of History*, awarded the *Los Angeles Times* Book Award. She is also the editor of the anthology *Against Forgetting: Twentieth Century Poetry of Witness*. Recently, she was presented with the Edita and Ira Morris Hiroshima Foundation Award for Peace and Culture in Stockholm. She lives in Maryland with her husband and son.